BOGN AT WAR

C000179239

Andy Saunders

MP Middleton Press

**Dedicated to Frank L'Alouette,
photographer, and to twenty-two
civilians who died in Bognor Regis as the
result of enemy action in 1939 - 45.**

*Front Cover: Bren Gun Carriers trundle past The Arcade during a
parade for War Weapons Week in 1941. The Chairman of Bognor
Regis Urban District Council and a senior Army Officer take the
salute and interested observers gape from first floor windows!*

First published November 1995

ISBN 1 873793 59 6

© Middleton Press 1995

Design - Deborah Goodridge

*Published by Middleton Press
Easebourne Lane
Midhurst
West Sussex
GU29 9AZ
Tel: 01730 813169
Fax: 01730 812601*

*Printed & bound by Biddles Ltd,
Guildford and Kings Lynn*

CONTENTS

	CAPTION NOS.	PAGE NOS.
1. The Photographer - Frank L'Alouette	1 - 3	4
2. Preparations for War	4 - 23	8
3. Battle of Britain	24 - 35	20
4. Battle over Bognor	36 - 38	26
5. The Air Raids	39 - 71	29
6. People, Places and Events	72 - 105	52
7. Victory at Last	106 - 116	74
8. Independence Day at Downview Road	117	90
9. Bognor Airfield	118	91
10. Flying Bomb Incident	119	92
11. The bombers return ... 1994.	120	93
Bognor's Civilian Roll of Honour		94
The Statistics		95
Aircraft losses		95

Street Map of Bognor Regis as it appeared during the immediate pre-war period.

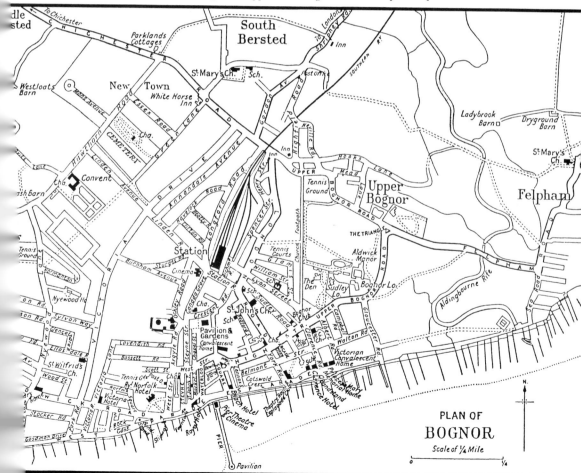

PLAN OF
BOGNOR
Scale of ¼ Mile

INTRODUCTION

In common with every seaside town on the South Coast, Bognor Regis came under frequent German air attack and suffered, too, the other hardships of wartime Britain between the years 1939 and 1945. During this period photography of events of every description was severely restricted by The Control of Photography Regulations and, of course, by shortages of film and materials. For both of these reasons there was only a limited amount of photography taking place in either an official or private capacity. Official photographers had to work under permit and private photographers were prohibited from taking pictures of any military significance. This meant that private snaps of bomb damage, crashed aeroplanes or of military establishments were, officially, illegal and historians must rely largely on archives of "approved" photographs which were controlled and regulated by the Ministry of Information. Many of these pictures were often artificially posed, or else the end product was heavily sanitised and censored to make the pictures acceptable for publication in the security-minded news media and for the propaganda or morale boosting efforts of the Ministry of Information. To a large extent these factors add up to a less than complete record of certain wartime events and places and it is therefore most interesting to be able to view almost the entire wartime history of one British town through the lens of one photographer. That town, is Bognor Regis and the photographer, Frank Lalouette, to whom this book is dedicated.

Frank L'Alouette's pictures provide a fascinating insight into almost every aspect of wartime life in Bognor and its environs. Some of the pictures were posed but many were taken, for example, as the dust settled after bombing attacks and the shaken residents emerged from their blasted homes or dug in the rubble for bodies or survivors. We are grateful to the family of Frank L'Alouette, and particularly to Mrs. Jenny Hickman, for making the publication of these pictures possible. Primarily, the photographs here were all taken by Frank and are a tribute both to him and the people of Bognor who endured and suffered those wartime years. In compiling these pictures, and in researching the captions, the author has not intended to offer a comprehensive wartime history of the town but to present a unique photographic image of some of the events, people and places in front-line Bognor Regis.

ACKNOWLEDGEMENTS

In compiling this album a very special thanks must go to Mrs. Jenny Hickman for making possible the publication of her late father's wonderful photographs. Without her help and wholehearted support and enthusiasm this book would have been quite impossible.

I am especially grateful to Alan Readman at the West Sussex Records Office and also to Martin Hayes of the West Sussex Library Service. Thanks also to Pat Burgess, Ian Hutton and Flt. Lt. Chris Goss.

To Vic Mitchell and Deborah Goodridge of Middleton Press I extend my thanks for their invaluable input towards producing this unique record.

Thanks also go to Trevor, Stella, and Gayle Linford for their invaluable work in preparing the text.

A friend of many years, Nancy Woodall, provided much valuable local information and helped to pinpoint certain locations and identified many of the places in the photographs. Thank you Nancy!

The "Bognor Regis Observer" have also been helpful and they are credited with the final photograph in this book. Thanks also to Dave Packham for additional photographic help.

Last, but by no means least, my wife Julie who helped with the preparation work and in the almost impossible task of selecting 120 photographs out of the hundreds available from Frank's collection. Thank you Julie!

1. THE PHOTOGRAPHER -
FRANK L'ALOUETTE

Born in Windsor, Berkshire, on 2nd February 1901, Frank was to become well known as a quality photographer in his adopted town of Bognor Regis and many will still remember his photographers shop at 32 West Street. By great good fortune many of Frank's wartime photographs of Bognor survive locally with members of his family and it has therefore been possible to draw upon that source to produce this book as a tribute to Frank L'Alouette the photographer.

After serving an apprenticeship as photographers assistant in Windsor, the young Frank moved to Bognor during the 1920s to work in the photographic department of Cleeves the Chemists in the High Street. From here, and having built up a considerable working knowledge of all things photographic, Frank felt sufficiently confident to branch out on his own during the late 1920s.

At this particular period, the Brownie Box Camera was at the height of its popularity and it was, without doubt, an essential piece of equipment for every holidaymaker. Recognising this, and with Bognor an increasingly popular resort, Frank L'Alouette was able to capitalise on the popularity of photography for everyone and bought his West Street premises in 1931. From here he built up a thriving local business as a general photographer - commercial, press, portraiture, weddings etc. as well as a camera and photographic requisite retailer. In addition, he had the bread and butter line of developing and printing. In this capacity, Frank was able to offer what was then a novelty - a same day developing and printing service which proved a great success with visiting holidaymakers. He also provided a developing and printing service for local chemists, collecting and delivering films for processing around the town and in outlying areas. Often, he would work around the clock to deal with the films that had been left at his shop or contracted out to him by local chemists.

Frank L'Alouette met his wife, Doris (nee Gray), in Bognor and they married at St. John's Church on 30th October 1927. At first, Doris helped with the busy shop but then a family came along and Frank was left largely on his own to operate the business. Daughters Jeanette, Pamela and Susan were born into the

L'Alouette family and the two eldest daughters appear in a number of Frank's wartime pictures.

With the outbreak of war, it was inevitable that both seaside holidays and recreational photography would all but cease and this would be catastrophic for many such businesses as that run by the L'Alouette's from West Street. However, Frank had aspirations to join the services but failed his medical when a previously undetected heart defect was identified. Indeed, it turned out that Frank had a hole-in-the-heart condition which clearly precluded any military service. Dejected, Frank realised he had to make what he could of his photographic business under wartime conditions but quickly sought a Ministry of Information Permit to enable him to photograph wartime events in and around Bognor Regis.

Frank's photography of wartime events was prolific, and he was often on the scene of incidents almost as soon as they happened. For him, there was never any shortage of film, glass plates, developing and printing chemicals or paper due to his work as an approved Ministry of Information photographer. All of his requirements were seen to by a regularly visiting Kodak representative.

When bombs fell, it was plainly obvious what had been hit and where - so it was only a matter of moments before he had grabbed his equipment and was on his way to the scene to shoot whatever there was to see with his trusty VN Press Camera; the results provided to local newspapers, and via Planet News Agency in London, for a wider distribution. Often, however, the censor would not approve the pictures and they would never see the light of day. Obviously there was a security requirement for this procedure, but more than fifty years on it is frustrating to realise that a pictorial record of certain events has been lost because of wartime censorship. All the same, Frank managed to compile a fascinating insight into wartime Bognor - as evidenced by this album. Wartime service in the local ARP also helped Frank's "intelligence gathering" of what to photograph and where. So, too, did a friendly relationship with the local constabulary who would often feed him a tip on where to be with his camera!

Despite this, the bread and butter Brownie Box Camera trade had gone. True, there was still an income from portrait sittings - very often of local young men and women in their service uniforms. There was also the income from photographs submitted for press use but, to supplement this, Frank displayed photographs of the local wartime events in his West Street shop window and offered prints for sale to interested residents. One wonders how many Frank L'Alouette prints are still in private hands in Bognor? Are there any out there which do not appear in this book? If so, Frank's family, the author and doubtless the West Sussex Records Office would like to know! Copies of many of the photographs are held by the Records Office but we know for certain that many have not been accounted for.

Surviving the rigours (and bombs!) of wartime Bognor, Frank was to continue running his photographic business post war. Latterly, he became a Director of L.B.L. Photographic in Scott Street before finally hanging up his camera in about 1956 and passing the photography business on to Mr. Charles Stevens.

Frank L'Alouette died in 1968, and those who knew him will recall a warm, friendly man who was cheerful, resourceful and energetic in his work. Part of his legacy is this remarkable "snap-shot" of life in wartime Bognor Regis. It has been a privilege to present his work in this format.

Andy Saunders. August 1995.

1. Frank L'Alouette, the photographer and family man. Here, he is pictured with his daughters, Jenny (left) and Pamela.

2. Frank L'Alouette's photographic shop and studios were situated in West Street before and during the war years. This 1930's shot shows a shop window sign advertising "Films left before Eleven, ready at Seven". Obviously a same-day service is nothing new!

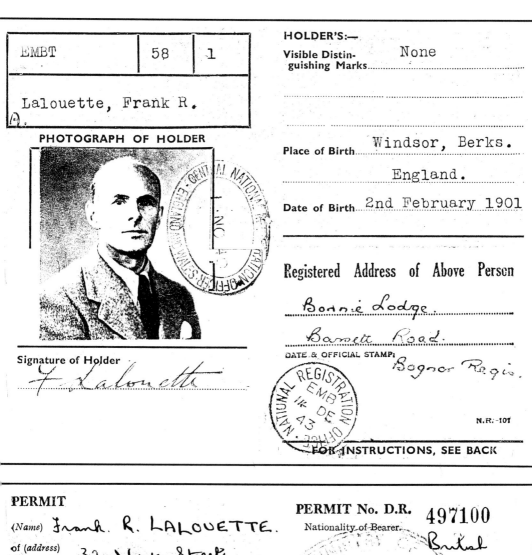

EMBT	58	1

Lalouette, Frank R.

PHOTOGRAPH OF HOLDER

Signature of Holder

F. Lalouette

HOLDER'S:—

Visible Distin-guishing Marks .... None

Place of Birth .... Windsor, Berks. England.

Date of Birth .... 2nd February 1901

Registered Address of Above Person

Bonnie Lodge.

Barrett Road.

DATE & OFFICIAL STAMP *Bognor Regis.*

N.R.-101

FOR INSTRUCTIONS, SEE BACK

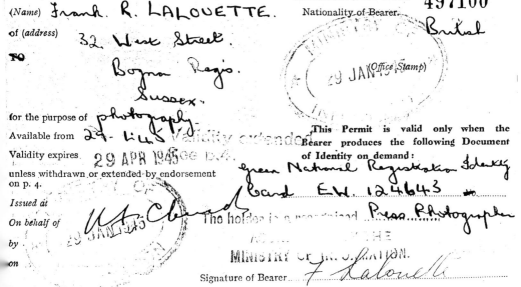

PERMIT

(Name) *Frank R. LALOUETTE.*

of (address) *32 West Street.*

TO *Bognor Regis. Sussex.*

for the purpose of *photography*

Available from *29-1-45*

Validity expires 29 APR 1945

unless withdrawn or extended by endorsement on p. 4.

Issued at

On behalf of

by

on

PERMIT No. D.R. 497100

Nationality of Bearer *British*

(Office Stamp) 29 JAN 45

This Permit is valid only when the Bearer produces the following Document of Identity on demand: *green National Registration Identity card EW 124643*

The holder is a recognised Press Photographer

MINISTRY OF INFORMATION.

Signature of Bearer *F. Lalouette*

2. PREPARATIONS FOR WAR

4. With war clouds looming in the summer of 1939, Mrs. L'Alouette and her two daughters take a picnic which is somewhat hindered by their gas masks! The new Morris 8 served as the photographer's car throughout the war.

5. More used to making sandcastles these youngsters help fill sandbags on Bognor beach during August 1939. For most it would be the last seaside holiday for a long while and the last opportunity to play on the beach for nearly six years.

6. More sandbags, more child labour! This time it is the main Post Office which is the focus of attention. For the children it is just exciting fun, but the policeman's tin hat adds a new dimension to these changing and dramatic times.

7. Fear of a gas attack was prevalent when war was declared on 3rd September 1939. In the event, poison gas was never used but gas attack exercises in London Road and High Street tested the readiness of the population to withstand such unpleasantness.

GAS ATTACK

HOW TO PUT ON YOUR GAS MASK

Always keep your gas mask with you – day and night. Learn to put it on quickly. Practise wearing it.

1. Hold your breath. 2. Hold mask in front of face, with thumbs inside straps.
3. Thrust chin well forward into mask, pull straps over head as far as they will go.
4. Run finger round face-piece taking care head-straps are not twisted.

IF THE GAS RATTLES SOUND

1. Hold your breath. Put on mask wherever you are. Close window.

2. If out of doors, take off hat, put on your mask. Turn up collar.

3. Put on gloves or keep hands in pockets. Take cover in nearest building.

IF YOU GET GASSED

BY VAPOUR GAS Keep your gas mask on even if you feel discomfort
If discomfort continues go to First Aid Post

BY LIQUID or BLISTER GAS

1	2	3	4
Dab, but *don't rub* the splash with handkerchief. Then destroy handkerchief.	Rub No. 2 Ointment well into place. *(Buy a 6d. jar now from any chemist).* In emergency chemists supply Bleach Cream free.	If you can't get Ointment or Cream within 5 minutes wash place with soap and warm water	Take off at once any garment splashed with gas.

PRINTED FOR H.M. STATIONERY OFFICE BY FOSH & CROSS LTD., LONDON   (51/504)

8. Schoolboys test their respirators in the "gas" outside the International Stores. Note that the destinations on the bus stop have been painted out for security reasons.

9. This was the east side of London Road during the gas attack exercise. Thankfully, the population of Great Britain were never subjected to gas attack and, consequently, did not have to don their gas masks for real. The threat of attack was ever present, though.

10. Road signs of all kinds were removed in what was both a security move and a drive for scrap metal. Place names were all obliterated so as not to aid the enemy, but leaving confused or lost travellers to be treated with immense suspicion if they asked their whereabouts! Here, a keep left bollard is taken away for scrap.

EVACUATION
OF
WOMEN AND CHILDREN
FROM LONDON, Etc.

FRIDAY, 1st SEPTEMBER.

Up and Down business trains as usual, with few exceptions.

Main Line and Suburban services will be curtailed while evacuation is in progress during the day.

SATURDAY & SUNDAY.
SEPTEMBER 2nd & 3rd.

The train service will be exactly the same as on Friday

Remember that there will be very few Down Mid-day business trains on Saturday.

SOUTHERN RAILWAY

With the outbreak of war imminent thousands of evacuees began to arrive in West Sussex to escape the feared bombing of London. During the first few days of September, 1939, trainloads of children were brought into Bognor Regis and the surrounding district. This was the poster displayed by Southern Railway at Bognor Station. When the bombing actually started in 1940, and with invasion likely, it became apparent that the South Coast was not a safe place for evacuees and they were re-evacuated.

11. ARP or Air Raid Precautions attracted a good number of volunteers for service. Here, the extinguishing of an Incendiary bomb by stirrup pump is demonstrated to the citizens of Bognor.

12. A requisitioned cafe by the Sands Hotel serves as mess hut for fresh army recruits still in their civilian clothes and under the watchful eye of a Sgt. P.T. Instructor. The culinary delights of Army life await!

13. "The Battle of France is over, the Battle of Britain is about to begin". So said Prime Minister Winston Churchill as rapid defence preparations for an expected invasion of England got under way. Here, a policeman guards access to the beaches which were now prohibited places. His colleague waits and watches to seaward.

14. Another of Churchill's famous lines comes to mind here. "We will fight them on the beaches...." could be the only caption to this picture as infantrymen train on the sands at Bognor during the early summer of 1940.

15. The serious business of rifle practice becomes fun and games for these two youngsters who eagerly and enthusiastically enter into the spirit of things with their pop-guns!

16. Bayonet practice, too, was carried out on the beaches which, in this picture, have not yet been closed to public access. Children enjoy the last days of sun and sand before the war finally comes to Bognor.

17. Up goes the wire. Miles of defensive barbed wire entanglements were strung out along Britain's seafronts and Bognor was no exception. These rusty and lethal fences were to remain in place for more than four years.

18. Not only were the entanglements to keep the enemy out but they also effectively kept the public off the beaches. In this classic picture the two L'Alouette girls gaze wistfully through the wire clutching their buckets and spades.

19. Two 5.5 inch guns were set up on the seaward side of gardens in Aldwick Avenue and here men of the Royal Artillery manhandle the barrel of one of the guns into position.

20. From here the gun would be capable of firing armour-piercing shells at ships seven miles off the shore in the event of German invasion. Already the neat garden has been transformed by barbed wire and military equipment. This was a town now very much in the front-line!

21. A little further away, another gun emplacement under camouflage netting has been set up in Sherwood Road. Smoke drifts away from the muzzle to the top left whilst the soldier on the right protects his ears against the percussion of firing.

22. Fuses for the Sherwood Road gun are set by Royal Artillerymen but at this stage of the war there was a shortage of ammunition and these guns were limited to only about 50 rounds each. Had invasion come then the defence of Britain would surely have been a desperate affair.

23. Concrete tank traps and defensive pill-boxes complete "Fortress Bognor" as the Duke of Gloucester makes a tour of the defences along the sea front. It is hard to imagine now just how the front was transformed in preparation for anticipated battle.

3. BATTLE OF BRITAIN

24. The districts first real taste of war came on 16th August 1940, when German "Stuka" dive bombers raided RA Tangmere. Here, smoke billows from the bombed out hangars in a picture captioned as "Taken looking North from Colworth".

25. Some of the Tangmere raiders paid a heavy price, however. Here, one of the "Stukas" has come to rest in a rathe battered state at Bowley Farm, South Mundham. Inevitably, a crowd comes to stare.

26. Two days after Tangmere was hit, the "Stukas" raided RAF Ford. Geysers of flame and acrid black smoke billow from blazing aircraft and wrecked transport close to one of the smashed hangars.

27. Aftermath. Survivors pick amongst the debris of flattened huts at Ford following the raid which left many dead and injured. In the space of two days residents of Bognor had witnessed the near destruction of their two neighbouring aerodromes at Tangmere and Ford.

28. On 26th August 1940, with the Battle of Britain reaching its height, Sgt. Pilot Cyril Babbage was shot down in his Spitfire off Bognor. After taking to his parachute, he was rescued by rowing boat.

29. Coming ashore he was met by local Policemen and Soldiers. Here, he has a cigarette lit for him before returning to his unit, 602 Squadron, based at Westhampnett. Note that the centre section has been removed from the pier to prevent its use as a landing stage by the Germans.

30. On 9th September 1940, a Junkers 88 bomber was shot down into the sea off Pagham. With the bomber partly submerged, the surviving crew members were taken off by rowing boat.

31. When the tide went out the bullet riddled bomber with its diving eagle emblem was the subject of close scrutiny. A soldier points out bullet holes in the front of the cockpit which indicated a head-on attack by the RAF fighter responsible for shooting down the bomber.

2. For this crewman of the Junkers 88, an ambulance as too late. The photograph was displayed in Frank 'Alouette's shop window but had to be removed when omplaints were made to the police about its content.

33. Using his can opener, a soldier removes the bullet holed swastika from the tail of the Pagham Junkers 88. One wonders where this interesting souvenir is today! Does anyone know?

4. BATTLE OVER BOGNOR

34. An RAF Airman carries ashore the bombsight from the Junkers 88 at Pagham Harbour. Technical equipment such as this was highly valuable for British Intelligence Officers who examined each shot down German aeroplane.

35. Flying Officer John Cutts of Felpham was the son of a well known local solicitor and was lost flying a Spitfire during the Battle of Britain. John vanished on 4th September 1940, and is still officially listed as "Missing in Action", although subsequent research has proven that his Spitfire crashed near Maidstone.

The Battle of Britain was all but over, but on 15th November 1940, a dogfight high above Bognor sent a Messerschmitt 109 flaming onto the beach at Felpham. By any standards it was a dramatic episode, and this is an account of that battle. More than fifty years on it is difficult to say with absolute certainty which RAF pilot actually sent the Messerschmitt crashing to the ground, but Combat Reports of the participants are available for examination. In addition, we have the benefit of a post-war account written by the Messerschmitt 109 pilot, Gefreiter Rudolf Miese. 15th November 1940, saw the Spitfires of 74 Squadron airborne from Biggin Hill whilst, from Tangmere, the Hurricanes of 213 Squadron joined up for an interception over the West Sussex coastline. Hearing a shout in his earphones of "Messerschmitts behind!" Sgt. Pilot Glendinning of 74 Squadron realised his section was about to be jumped. In his official Combat Report he wrote:-

"An Me.109 went past me on my port side. I delivered a beam attack. He flipped over on his back and, for a few seconds, seemed to hang in the air. I again closed in and gave him another burst. Pieces flew in all directions, and he went down in a series of rolls. Still not being satisfied, I gave another burst and something seemed to explode inside the machine and the tail came away. The Me.109 disappeared into the sea near Bognor Regis."

The facts as reported by Sgt. Glendinning are very precise and fit, quite neatly, with the known details of the wrecked Messerschmitt. Indeed, an RAF Intelligence Officer reported "....aircraft crashed in shallow water in the sea at Felpham. Only the rear end of the fuselage and tailplane was found, but examination of this pointed to an explosion in the air." Proof positive, one may think, that this was certainly the machine destroyed by Glendinning. But another report by Flying Officer Gould of 213 Squadron also lays claim to the same Messerschmitt:-

"I saw an Me.109 coming down in a shallow dive above me and in front. I turned towards the enemy aircraft in a starboard turn. The 109 increased dive and I delivered a quarter attack, saw bullets hit machine but lost enemy in almost vertical dive. Broke off engagement and returned to base reporting probable enemy loss

Afterwards, enemy aircraft was reported to have crashed at Felpham, pilot baling out."

Rudolf Miese, the Messerschmitt pilot, can obviously throw no light on who the victor was. However, his account of events makes interesting reading:-

"I was flying with 4/JG.2 on 15th November 1940 and had taken off from Le Havre under the leadership of Ltn. Julius Meimberg. Shortly before reaching the English coast we spotted, coming from the left and below, a formation of 12 to 15 Spitfires. Uffz Dessoy and myself swung to the left and attacked the English from the front and above. I do not know whether I hit the machine I attacked or not, but it rolled and dived away. We were already below the sun when we pulled back to the left but then, from above and the left and behind the cockpit, I was hit by tracer. Immediately, the aircraft burst into flames and dived. Simultaneously I threw off the cockpit roof and undid my straps. Then I lost consciousness and must have fallen out. Luckily, the parachute opened. As consciousness returned I hung about 2000 metres up swinging on my parachute quite strongly. I was without flying boots or socks, there was a hole in my life jacket and I was still over the water but not far from the coast. My hands and face were burnt and my left arm was smashed. Two British aircraft circled and the pilots waved to me. I was blown by the wind nearer the coast and landed on a road close to a beach without injuring myself further. About twenty civilians and a Bobby came running. The policeman rolled up the parachute and pulled it away from my body. Then, an RAF Doctor appeared and gave me first aid, bandaging my arm in the street. I was then rushed by ambulance to hospital in Littlehampton where I had three operations on my arm. When I came round after the first operation after I being taken prisoner, an RAF Intelligence Officer was by the side of my bed. He interrogated me and reproached me for carrying my operational pilots pass and then went on to name my C.O, Senior Officers and all the pilots of 4/JG2 - as well as our airfield at Beaumont Le Roger and the operational fields at Cherbourg and Le Havre! He even told me our take off times that day. I remained in hospital at Littlehampton until March 1941 and during that time my kindly RAF Doctor twice came to visit me." Rudolf Miese's escapade at Bognor was not untypical of events during the Battle of Britain period, but it was an event which left indelible memories on

those citizens of Bognor who witnessed it. It is unfortunate, however, that no photos seem to have been taken of the tail section where it fell in the Crossbush Road area........or perhaps someone has one hidden away somewhere? Maybe, as well, somebody picked up a souvenir or two of that Battle over Bognor?

36. The graceful beauty of vapour trails traced against an azure blue sky belied the true nature of the life-and-death struggle which they represented when RAF and German fighter aircraft tangled in mortal combat. Here, Frank L'Alouette has captured the scene as Messerschmitts, Spitfires and Hurricanes engage in the dramatic dogfight over Bognor on 15th November 1940.

37. Sgt. John Glendinning, a Spitfire pilot serving with 74 Squadron, was probably responsible for shooting down Rudolf Miese over Felpham on 15th November 1940. In March of the following year, this 28 year old pilot was himself shot down by Messerschmitt 109s and died when his aircraft crashed on Romney Marsh, Kent.

38. Messerschmitt 109 pilot Rudolf Miese was lucky to escape with his life when he parachuted from his stricken fighter high above Bognor on 15th November 1940. Badly wounded he landed in a roadway somewhere near the beach at Felpham.

5. THE AIR RAIDS

39. The first bombs in Bognor fell on 14th September 1940, when eight high explosives fell at around quarter past three in the afternoon, from Sudley Lodge, across The Den and to Knights Corner. This was the scene at The Den which took a direct hit. Eleven year old Stanley Scowen and eighteen year old Leonard Dean both died in this air raid.

40. Lethal shrapnel has pock-marked the walls of the blasted buildings at Knights Corner which have been pictured through a hole in the flint wall, made by the falling bomb. Anyone this close to the explosion would have been cut to pieces and the effects of blast are clearly evident here.

41. Another view of damage caused during the Knights Corner incident. Firemen, policemen, air raid wardens and soldiers take stock of what has just happened here. It was an occurrence which was to become all too depressingly familiar over the next four years.

Air raids such as those of 14th September, 1940, no doubt prompted many residents of Bognor Regis to purchase the "Kendarp" air aid shelter as advertised by Ockendens of Littlehampton.

42. The next air raid of any significance took place on 27th December 1940, when fifteen 50Kg bombs were dropped from the Servite Convent to Hawthorn Road and across Chichester Road and Sherwood Avenue. This was the scene at Highland Avenue.

43. This is another view of the damage at Highland Avenue on 27th December 1940, where one of fifteen bombs wrecked this home. A few pathetic salvaged possessions rest on a rather battered table plonked on the rubble strewn lawn.

4. These two children had a lucky escape in the raid of 27th December. They have apparently managed to rescue some of their toys but it seems that the dolls, too, have been bombed-out of their battered dolls house!

45. At Chichester Road on 27th December, sixty year old Constance Addison was the only fatality in the raid. O[...]
half of this semi has been entirely flattened in an all too familiar and dismal scene.

46. On the night of 19th March 1941, sixteen H.E. bombs fell across Shripney Road north of the Gas Works a[...]d o[...]
dropped in soft ground failing to explode. The unexploded bomb, several feet beneath a kale field, was dealt with [...]
a Royal Engineer Bomb Disposal team.

47. This was the scene near the junction of Felpham Road (now Upper Bognor Road) and Felpham Way after bombs had fallen in the early hours of 9th April 1941. This view is taken looking towards Snook's Corner in the distance.

48. This is the same incident, but close to the junction with High Street. Two bombs exploded in this air raid incident, but one failed to detonate and buried itself in the grass verge close to the road. The "Danger, Unexploded Bomb" sign can just be made out below the shattered street lamp. This UXB was not made safe until th May, 1941 and the roads remained closed until 24th May.

49. With the night blitz at its peak, residential areas across England continued to suffer at the hands of the Luftwaffe. This was Annandale Avenue which caught one of the twenty four bombs dropped in a line from Hillsborough Road to London Road on the night of 11th April 1941. The street sweeper ruefully considers the task in hand!

50. Among the buildings damaged on 11th April 1941 were the printing works of the Bognor Post where the wreckage was photographed by Frank L'Alouette the next day, as Mr. Percy Long sweeps up.

52. Another view of the Pagham Road parachute mine incident as a removal van collects salvageable effects from the ruins. That anyone survived such close proximity to the explosion is little short of a miracle.

51. This was the result when two parachute mines exploded behind cottages on the south side of Pagham Road on 17th April 1941. Incredibly, the occupants of the houses were unhurt but Frank L'Alouette's notes record that "...Special Constable Hickman fell in the crater!"

53. On the night of 11th May 1941, fourteen bombs fell in a line across Shripney Road, the railway line and through the Bognor Regis Urban District Council's destructor works. This was the clearing up getting underway at the destructor works where a huge crater has been blasted with damage to the adjacent buildings.

54. The worst air raid suffered by Bognor took place on 14th August 1942, when four 250Kg bombs hit Burnham Avenue and Sturgess Road and a single 1000Kg exploded on 46 Sudley Road. It was at this latter incident that the worst casualties were experienced, although the total death toll for the raid reached nine. At Sudley Road at least one house had simply vanished into a huge crater.

55. This was the scene at Sudley Road as rescuers desperately tore at the rubble to free victims. Rescue work of this kind was, by its very nature, potentially very hazardous with the rescuers at danger from further collapse, unexploded bombs, gas and live cables.

56. At Burnham Avenue, a crowd gathers to gape at the debris and neighbours emerge to render what help they can. Seventy-eight year old Elizabeth Cronin was injured here and died the next day. This picture was taken moment after the bombs had fallen.

57. Further along Burnham Avenue a delivery woman with this bakers handcart had a remarkable escape as she sheltered beneath the cart when bombs started to fall. One of the 250Kg bombs cratered the road just yards away from her. As others inspect the scene an air raid warden checks off his casualty list.

58. This is a general view of the devastation caused in the Sudley Road incident. The widespread nature of damage caused by the effect of blast is clearly apparent in this picture.

59. On 17th September 1942, a low flying Focke Wulf 190 released a single 500Kg bomb which passed through o
of the gas holders at the gas works without exploding and then detonated on a bridge at Shripney Road. This was t
hole punched in the gasometer.

60. This was what happened when the deflected bomb exploded on the bridge over the Rife in Shripney Road on 17th September 1942 and set off landmines adding to the severity of damage. All through traffic was stopped until 25th September when a temporary bridge was constructed to the north-west of the demolished structure.

61. On the same day as the Shripney Road incident, another bomb hit the rear of West Parade Hotel and demolished Mill House. Firemen survey the scene and plan a search for survivors or for bodies.

62. The much battered gasworks actually had a German Dornier 217 fly straight into it on 16th December 1942, while taking evasive action when persued by an RAF fighter. The bomber first struck the tallest gas holder, leaving its wing inside, then fell into one of the smaller gas holders. All of the crew were killed.

63. The next day Frank L'Alouette photographed the gash in the wall of the gasholder from the inside. He was accompanied by a Board of Trade official, whose head and shoulders add scale.

4. The Gasworks Dornier was claimed by a Canadian Anti-Aircraft battery at Felpham. This Bofors gun crew only ~~~t off one round before their weapon jammed but, all the same, painted a swastika and date on the gun to mark ~~eir "claim".

HAROLD BOOKERS HOUSE, OUR HOUSE WAS RIGHT BEHIND

65. An unfortunate consequence of the Gasworks Dornier episode was that the stricken bomber released two bombs which fell on Victoria Drive and Havelock Road. Here, at Victoria Drive, Harold Booker and Georgina Hepton were both killed.

66. Also in Victoria Drive on 16th December 1942, the two Army officers in this car had what can only be described as a miraculous escape. The white bands on the tree were to aid driving in blackout conditions.

7. On 5th February 1943, a "Hit and Run" attack by four Focke Wulf 190s caused widespread damage and casualties. ...ne of four bombs went through a roof in Chapel Street, bounced, then exploded at the rear of the Merchant Taylor's ...ome. This was the badly damaged interior of the Merchant Taylor's Chapel.

68. After the 5th February 1943 raid the ritual of clearing up broken glass gets underway. Here, Ben Sarell (left) and the appropriately named Lewis Glasspool shovel up the shattered windows of Messrs. Reynolds and Co.

69. An ARP worker injured in the air raid of 5th February 1943 is given First Aid at Bognor Pavilion. The car has been pressed into service as an ambulance for walking wounded.

70. Madeline Hannyngton and Mildred Gooder were both casualties of the raid on 5th February 1943 and were fatally injured at Albert Road. This was one of the substantial houses ripped apart by lethal high explosive.

71. Casualty evacuation takes place along Albert Road in the aftermath of the 5th February attack. Willing hands carry an unfortunate victim past the junction with Walton Road.

72. Rationing was a fact of life in wartime Britain. Here, a queue forms at Messrs. J.W. Woodford in London Road as patient housewives endure a regular wartime routine. Fish was one of the few commodities not to be rationed and thus queues formed for the limited supplies available.

CLOTHING BOOK 1945-46 GENERAL CB 1/8

This book must not be used until the holder's name, full postal address and National Registration Number have been written below. Detach this book at once and keep it safely. It is your only means of buying clothing.

HOLDER'S NAME *D.W. LALOUETTE*
(in BLOCK letters)

ADDRESS *BONNIE LODGE*
(in BLOCK letters)
BASSETT RD, BOGNOR REGIS

HOLDER'S NATIONAL REGISTRATION No.
FMBT / 58 / 2

IF FOUND please take this book to any Food Office or Police Station

FOOD OFFICE CODE No.

FD/SE8

HOLD Pages I—VIII in one hand and
TEAR ALONG THIS LINE

THIS BOOK IS NUMBER
H 041864

PAGE I

It wasn't only food which was rationed. Clothing, too, could only be purchased by controlled coupons and commodities not on ration were, inevitably, in short supply.

73. A Bren Gun Carrier trundles past the Royal Norfolk Hotel. Military traffic and Army convoys became the norm, and apart from public transport and goods vehicles, there were very few private cars on the road during the war years. It is interesting to note the shadow of a horse on the roadway in the foreground.

74. "Wish you were here - Bognor, 1940!" A Senior Polish Army Officer and his British counterpart take a break from the arduous task of reviewing defences and tuck into an apparently well stocked picnic hamper.

75. More infantry training on the beach. This time a mortar is fired out to sea in what appears to be a demonstration for the troops. One or two nosey civilians peer through the barbed wire.

76. The London Irish Regiment were stationed in and around Bognor Regis for some while during the war years. This soldier was, inevitably, known to all as "Tiny". At 6ft 10ins he towered above his fellow squaddies!

77. The Regimental Band, and Irish Wolfhound mascot, were popular attractions for the local children. Here, Jenny and Pamela L'Alouette make friends with "Barney" outside The Theatre Royal complex.

78. The Regiment's splendid line in headgear is shown to advantage here as an officer and warrant officer con
outside the Clarence Hotel.

79. A local lad, Norman Reynolds, acts up for Frank L'Alouette's camera. Kitted out as an officer of the London Irish he is saluted by a passing troop of regimental soldiers on The Esplanade.

80. Take aim! The crew of a light field gun take a sight on a passing coaster from a position on the eastern end of the Esplanade as they practice to repel the expected German invasion during 1940.

81. Another view of the gun crew in action looking back westwards towards the pier with the Theatre Royal complex on the right. A group of officers look on.

82. "Eyes right!" Men of an infantry battalion march past the saluting base at the entrance to the Arcade during the March 1941 War Weapons Week. Pounds, shillings and pence for victory proclaims the sign which indicates a local fund raising target of 200,000.

83. War Weapons Week again. This time, an ARP demonstration is underway at the Pavilion as wardens clad in anti-gas clothing lower a volunteer "casualty" to the ground. The volunteer for this precarious exercise can only be described as somewhat heroic!

SUPPORT OUR WAR WEAPONS WEEK

84. This angelic toddler sits happily astride a British 250lb General Purpose bomb, liberally plastered with war savings stamps during one of the many was weapons fund initiatives in Bognor Regis. Do any of our readers recognise the child - or the venue?

5. This large model of a Royal Navy Motor Torpedo at was carried around Bognor Regis on the back of an AF trailer as part of the War Weapons Week fund ising initiative. Local fund raising targets were often ceeded in these great patriotic drives to help fund the r effort.

86. Captain Curry leads the Pagham Home Guard past the bombed out bungalow at Pagham Road (see also photos 51 and 52). Is that Corporal Jones bringing up the rear on his bicycle?!

87. "Halt! Identity Card please. What is the purpose of your journey?" Entry to all South Coast districts was strictly controlled and here troops man a road block. Private cars such as this Ford 8 were a comparative rarity in wartime Britain. Note that the soldiers have established a permanent sand-bagged dugout at this road junction on the outskirts of Bognor Regis.

88. Regular troops conduct an exercise which involves crossing The Rife without getting their feet wet - hopefully! Note the wooden posts in the far distance which were erected as an invasion countermeasure to prevent airborne troops making glider landings.

89. Police Sgt. William Avis of Bognor Police was shot dead by an unbalanced Canadian Army deserter, Pte John Moore, at Fernhurst Gardens on 26th February 1942. His cold blooded murder severely shook the town and resulted in a massive manhunt.

90. Armed police, home guardsmen and regular soldiers scoured the town and surrounding district for the murderer, who was known to be still armed and dangerous. In the event, however, he slipped the net and was finally arrested at South Mimms in Hertfordshire.

91. Brought back in handcuffs, Pte. John Moore was charged at Chichester and committed for trial at the Old Bailey. Moore was clearly unbalanced, and was found to be insane and not capable of standing trial.

92. On the night of 23rd/24th April 1942, a Hampden bomber crashed at the south end of Sea Road, Felpham, in a field behind some huts and burst into flames. The four crew were killed and six unexploded bombs found in the burnt out wreckage.

3. There was high drama at Bognor Gasworks on 3rd July 1942. Messerschmitt 109s had shot up the gas holders, puncturing them and setting them alight. As the fire brigade played hoses on the leaks gas company employees, Mr. W.R. Hammond (left) and Mr. H. Glazier (centre), plugged the bullet holes with wet clay. For this brave work Mr. Hammond was awarded the MBE and Mr. Glazier the BEM.

94. Well known on the radio, comedy duo Ethel and Doris Waters seem enthusiastic about whatever it is in the saucepan, "......somewhere in Bognor." The bystander seems a little bemused, but perhaps he is contemplating eating whatever it is in the enamel bowl - the contents of which look less than appealing!

96. "Save your waste paper and cardboard!" was one of the wartime salvage initiatives. Men of Bognor's Civil Defence Force help with the collection programme and are seen here in West Street. Obviously recycling is not a new idea!

5. On 22nd April 1943, Sgt. Pilot E.H.Fletcher of 197 Squadron lost his life when his Typhoon aircraft spun into the ground and crashed at Beatty Road. Firemen and other rescuers pick through the smouldering remains of the fighter which had unfortunately also killed Leonard Martlew in his garden and injured a Miss Daisy Smith of Havelock Road.

97. HM The Queen was a wartime visitor to Bognor and seemed radiantly cheerful as she chatted to local Girl Guides despite being in mourning for her brother-in-law, The Duke of Kent, who had been killed in a flying incident whilst serving in the RAF.

98. "Give us the tools and we'll finish the job" said Churchill. His call met with response from many small engineering plants, one of which was Jones' Garage in Belmont Street where these girls turned out 40,000 bullets a day, putting in long hours from dawn till mid-evening.

99. Down at the other end of Belmont Street, men of Bognor's Home Guard prepare to mount a mock-attack on the Town Hall as part of a training exercise. The front entrance has been bricked up and transformed into a surface air raid shelter. The S-22 sign says "Shelter Here" and signifies a capacity of 22 persons.

100. This scene was pictured outside The Tuck Shop at the junction of Upper Bognor Road (now High Street) and Gloucester Road. Exactly what is being played out here is uncertain, but presumably it is some kind of exercise by the Army in rounding up "Fifth Columnists." The building was demolished in 1968, but of historical note is the fact that it was here the future Queen Victoria is said to have purchased her first pair of boots, in about 1830!

102. Firewomen despatch riders ready for the off at Bognor Fire Station. With telephone communications unreliable in air raids, and little in the way of radio communication, the service of despatch riders to and from the scene of an incident was invaluable. Note the blackout masks on the bikes' headlights.

01. Firewomen of the National Fire Service run out oses from a trailer pump during a drill at Bognor Fire tation in 1943. The men stand and watch!

103. Bognor's Air Raid Wardens. Front row, fifth from right, is Head Warden Mr J.L.Surridge. Back row, extreme left is Warden L'Alouette! So who took the picture....?! The gas lamps were unused for years.

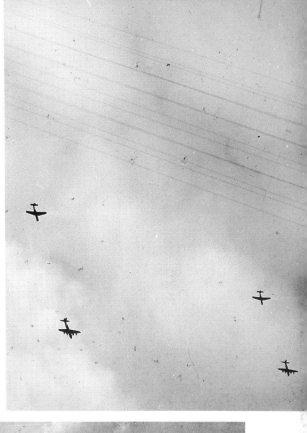

104. Along with all towns on the South Coast, Bognor Regis was caught up in the drama of D-Day on 6th June 1944. Overhead, masses of airborne assault gliders, towed by heavy aircraft, headed out for Normandy and were photographed from Bognor Regis by Frank L'Alouette.

105. Offshore, part of the massive armada for the sea-borne assault was also photographed by Frank. Photographs such as this would have been considered militarily very sensitive and publication would have been delayed for weeks - even if publication were allowed at all.

106. With the war in Europe over on 8th May 1945 (VE Day), crowds gathered in the High Street to dance to relayed music. Others just stood and watched and wondered how to feel now that a long wearying war was over.

107. Another view of the VE Day crowds in the High Street looking towards the bus station. The oblong brick building is a surface air raid shelter denoted by the "S" sign on the end wall. Thankfully, its days of usefulness were now past.

108. As night fell on VE Day celebration bonfires were lit the length and breadth of Britain. Here, crowds happily watch as an effigy of Adolf Hitler is consumed by the flames at the West End Car Park.

109. Street parties were held for children on VE Day, 8th May 1945. This one took place in Lyon Street against the background of St. John's and the cleared site of the Sudley Road incident. (See photo number 54).

110. The King declared Sunday 13th May 1945 as a day of National Thanksgiving. Here, a Civic Service is held in the Pavilion where the Vicar, the Rev. L.E. Meredith, quoted General Wolfe at Quebec: "Victory is ours. Oh, let us keep it." The flags of the Allied Nations hang above the congregation.

111. In the summer of 1945, the defences against invasion were gradually cleared away. Here, children lend a willin hand to remove barbed wire entanglements from the Esplanade. Many wartime children had never experienced day at the seaside and this photo contrasts markedly with picture number 17.

→

112. Other defences on the beaches consisted of scaffolding barricades, erected to obstruct any attempted landing seaborne forces. This picture was taken in 1945, and shows Prince Michael of Kent clambering on the defence wor while his sister, Princess Alexandra, watches. The scaffolding was finally taken down shortly afterwards.

113. Bognor's Victory Parade, May 1945. The stalwart men and women of the Civil Defence march past the saluting base in the High Street. Throughout the war years they had dealt with 82 air raids and countless other incidents, providing a permanently manned service for the protection of Bognor's civilian population.

114. This buoyant mine was washed ashore near the Carlton Hotel on October 1945 and wedged itself in the groyne - fortunately without exploding. It was dealt with by the Royal Navy Bomb & Mine Clearance Unit and was just one of many similar incidents which became the dangerous legacy of six years of war.

DIV. REF. WD/KME.   H.Q. REF. M.O.1683.

~~AIR RAID INCIDENT~~ (MISCELLANEOUS) OBJECT.

Parish   BOGNOR REGIS.   Date 23rd October, 1945.   Time 10.35 hours.

Nature of Incident   FOUND - BRITISH MINE.

DETAIL

At 10.35 hours on the 23rd October, 1945, a British mine was washed ashore at Bognor Regis, MR.357184. This was secured on beach and usual authorities were notified.

This mine was rendered safe at 15.45 hours the same day.

NOT ENTERED IN UX REGISTER.

Time and Date Information received by Police ....

Signature ....

This was the official report on the Carlton Hotel mine - a matter-of-fact statement about just another incident!

115. Sometimes, the disposal of sea mines which had been washed ashore ended with tragic results. Here, willing hands tend to Lt. Prior, RN, who had been fatally injured in the explosion of a mine he was dealing with on Bognor beach. Standing on the right is Mrs. Rank who had been administering first aid to the critically injured officer. This incident was at the end of Dark Lane.

16. Previously described as a VE Day party on 8th May 1945, we now believe this was a VJ Day celebration on 15th August 1945, somewhere in one of the outlying districts of Bognor Regis. The lightweight clothes and summer frocks seem to contrast with the heavier clothing being worn in pictures of VE Day events - for example, picture no. 109. Perhaps a reader will recognise the event and venue and confirm our deductions?

8. INDEPENDENCE DAY AT DOWNVIEW ROAD

On 4th July, 1944, a B-17 Flying Fortress of the United States Army Air Force which had been crippled by flak over France limped back to the English coast and made landfall at Bognor. Unable to make it to either Ford or Tangmere the bomber made a forced-landing at Downview Road, ending up just feet away from houses there. At number 18 Miss Ethel Cheney stood at the kitchen sink washing up her breakfast things only to find herself caught up in high drama. Here, she takes up her own story:

"I had been working away for the WVS as Welfare Officer for the evacuees and this was my first day back at home. It was about twenty past nine and looking out of the kitchen window I could see a plane circling overhead and then realised it was coming in to land. It touched down in the field behind my house, and as I watched I was horrified to see the plane thundering towards me. Riveted to the spot I covered my eyes and offered up a quick prayer for protection. Realising I was still alive I nervously took away my hands and was amazed at the sight which met my eyes. The aeroplane had come to rest in my garden and when it was only about 50 feet from my house it had turned through 90 degrees and stopped with its wing tip six feet from my back door. All of the crew had jumped out, and were dancing, shouting and cheering on my lawn. I dried my hands and went down the path towards them. "Would you boys like some tea?" I asked. "Coffee would be better!" came the reply. So, they all came into my kitchen where we had coffee. Only two of the crew were hurt, one having had his shoulder dislocated in the crash and another had some shrapnel wounds around his waist. However, it was Independence Day so they all trooped back into my rather transformed garden and set off all the flares they had in the aeroplane! That night a plane arrived at Tangmere to take them back to their home base, although it took three weeks for the aeroplane to be dismantled and removed. All in all, those American boys and I had had a very lucky and narrow escape. Independence Day always brings back special memories for me. Doubtless it does, too, for "my" American boys - and one of them has dropped in to see me since. On 4th July, 1969, exactly twenty five years to the day, Mayo R. Adams Jr, the pilot, came back and took tea with me!"

Today, it is hard to visualise the big four engined bomber sitting on the lawns in Downview Road attracting hordes of sight-seers and souvenir hunters. How many pieces of the bomber survive today in garden sheds and attics around Bognor, and how many people have even the remotest inkling that this dramatic episode took place here?

117. This was the scene at the end of Miss Cheney's garden in Downview Road on 4th July, 1944, when Mayo Adams landed his crippled B-17 Flying Fortress. The occupants of both plane and houses had a remarkably lucky escape.

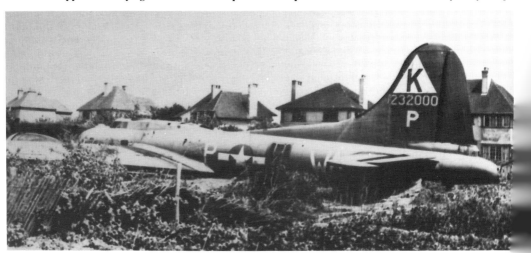

9. BOGNOR AIRFIELD

Officially designated an Advanced Landing Ground the airfield at Bognor was established near Rose Green at Morells Farm where it straddled the B2166. It came into use on 1st June, 1943, under control of RAF Tangmere, its "parent" station. In the lead-up to D-Day Bognor ALG became home to a number of Spitfire squadrons. At the end of March, 1944, 66 Squadron arrived along with two Norwegian Squadrons, 331 and 332. Flying from Bognor, this latter squadron met with notable success over France on 11th April when it destroyed six aircraft on an airfield near Paris. Accommodation at Bognor ALG was spartan, being mostly under canvas. However, this familiarised air and ground crews with the conditions they were about to experience in the push across Europe. Some, though, were lucky and were billeted in various homes around Bognor Regis and in the nearby West Meads estate. With the operational squadrons moving out by the end of June, 1944, 83 Group Support Unit moved in. This organisation held reserve stocks of replacement pilots and aircraft to fill gaps caused by operational losses in Europe. Over 100 aircraft of all the front-line fighter types flooded into Bognor, along with ambulance Avro Ansons which ferried blood plasma into Normandy and casualties out. At Bognor, too, there were casualties. For example, on the 11th September 1944 a Mustang with an engine fire making an emergency landing collided with another taking off from thr opposite direction. One of the pilots was killed. By November, 1944, the site was no longer needed and the perforated steel tracking which formed the two runways was torn up and the four corrugated iron "blister" hangars dismantled. Only a few concrete hardstandings remained to show what had once taken place here. Today, building development has encroached on the ALG and the rest has reverted to farmland. Here and there one will see gaps in hedgerows left by wartime runways or taxi-ways. If one searches harder it is still possible to find one or two sections of the perforated and inter-locking steel tracking which made up the runways. Otherwise, few would ever know of the existence of Bognor ALG or the important part it played as just one of the springboards for Operation Overlord, the invasion of Normandy.

118. Immediately after D-Day, a few Spitfire aircraft were used to fly English beer out to the invasion forces. The beer was put into modified auxiliary fuel tanks and here a Norwegian fighter pilot watches as the unusual "fuel" is put aboard. This picture has sometimes been described as taken at Tangmere. However, the presence of a Norwegian pilot would seem to suggest Bognor as the location, since No. 132 (Norwegian) Wing were based there over the D-Day period.

10. THE FLYING BOMB INCIDENT

The majority of V1 Flying Bombs which fell in the country came down in South East England, but mostly on a line to the East of Seaford. V1 incidents in West Sussex were therefore something of a rarity, but on 27th August, 1944, at 7.15 in the morning, one of these missiles exploded between Shelley Road and Tennyson Road. Unfortunately we have been unable to trace photographs of this event which proved to be the last wartime bomb incident in Bognor. One who witnessed the episode, however, was Nancy Woodall. Here is her account. "My mother, together with my brothers and my Aunt, lived in Shelley Road. I was staying that week with a friend, Miss Kitty Butt, at 26 Tennyson Road. I had just finished dressing and was looking out of the bedroom bay window. A steady harsh buzz and a V1 flew past, so close it was almost at roof height. Then, the engine cut out. I dived away from the window and there was a terrific explosion. The "return wave" of the blast must have caught me because I found myself lying up against the far wall, two inter-connecting rooms and a long landing away. Chairs and a heap of lighter furniture were piled up, on, and around me. I got up slowly. I was uninjured - though later I found the pocket watch and fountain pen smashed to bits in my uniform tunic pocket. I had a fine crop of bruises, too! I ran across to Shelley Road - in the distance all I could see around our house was dust and smoke. As I got close my mother walked slowly towards me. "We've had a bomb, dear" she said. I put my arm out to her and found tangled in the pocket of her cardigan a jagged 4 inch sliver of metal shrapnel. My brothers then appeared, and then my Aunt. All shaken, but miraculously unhurt. Had they still been in their bedrooms they wouldn't have stood a chance. We were not allowed back into the remains of the house, but one thing caught my eye. The long pendulum of the grandfather clock was standing upright, deeply embedded in a floor board. We had three very dear ducks and had built them a small concrete domed Duck Shelter. I found it deep in rubble but we prised off the heavy block at the back. Three dusty ducks, quackless with shock but otherwise unhurt, were carried to a nearby tennis court. Tragically, very many houses were badly damaged and many people injured. We had so much to be thankful for". According to the official record 65 people were injured in the Flying Bomb incident, 4 houses were demolished, 9 seriously damaged and 550 slightly damaged. The same record also states there was one fatality. However, if this is correct the casualty cannot be identified in the War Graves Commission Roll of Civilian War Dead. The Shelley Road V1 is recorded as Bognor's Air Raid Incident No. 82. It was also Bognor's last bomb. Well......almost.

119. The V1 Flying Bomb, or "Doodlebug", was a comparatively rare visitor to West Sussex, but on 27th August 1944 one fell between Shelley Road and Tennyson Road. Widespread damage and casualties resulted from the terrific explosion.

11. THE BOMBERS RETURN ... 1994

120. Bognor's last bomb. Almost exactly fifty years to the day after the final wartime bomb incident in Bognor, the IRA detonated a bomb in London Road precinct. It proved to be the last IRA terrorist bomb on mainland Britain before the 1994 cease-fire. One can only hope it will be Bognor's last bomb ever.

The author would be pleased to hear from anyone having photographs of wartime events in Sussex, most particularly relating to bombing or wartime aircraft losses in the county. Andy Saunders may be contacted via Tangmere Military Aviation Museum (see back page).

ROLL OF CIVILIAN WAR DEAD FOR THE URBAN DISTRICT OF BOGNOR REGIS

ADDISON, CONSTANCE LOUISE, age 60; of Fircroft, Chichester Road. Daughter of the late Revd William Addison, M.A., of Warrenford Manse, Chathill, Northumberland. 27 December 1940, at Fircroft, Chichester Road.

BOOKER, HAROLD NUTCOMBE, age 65; of Barton, Victoria Drive. 16 December 1942, at Bognor Regis War Memorial Hospital.

CRIPPS, ELSIE KATHLEEN, age 47; of 38 Annandale Avenue. 12 April 1941, at Bognor Regis War Memorial Hospital.

CRONIN, ELIZABETH, age 78; of Country Side, Burnham Avenue. Daughter of John Cronin, of Co. Waterford, Irish Republic. Injured 14 August 1942, at Bognor Regis; died 15 August 1942, at Bognor Regis War Memorial Hospital.

DEAN, LEONARD ROBERT, age 18. Son of Mrs. M. Dean, of Ockley Road. Injured 14 September 1940, at Sudley Lodge; died 15 September 1940, at Bognor Regis War Memorial Hospital.

FORD, ALICE, age 68; of Dunnett Road, Cheriton, Folkstone, Kent. Widow of Frederick Ford. 17 September 1942, at Wilsdon, Goodman Drive.

FRY, FANNY MARY ANN, age 65; of Wilsdon, Goodman Drive. Widow of John Fry. Injured 17 September 1942, at Wilsdon, Goodman Drive; died 27 October 1942, at 13 Newtown Avenue.

GOODER, MILDRED ALICE, age 51; of Seacroft, Albert Road. Daughter of Albert Gooder. 7 February 1943, at Bognor Regis War Memorial Hospital.

GRAPES, ELIZA, age 79; of Sudley House, Sudley Road. Widow of Henry Grapes. 14 August 1942, at Sudley Road.

HANNYNGTON, MADELINE GORDON, age 59; of Shorebank, Albert Road. Daughter of Brig.-Gen. Forbes and Edith Forbes; widow of Frank Hannynton. 5 February 1943, at Shorebank, Albert Road.

HAYHURST, LILLIAN, age 60; of 2 Sudley Road. Widow of Major J. Hayhurst. 14 August 1942, at Sudley Road.

HEPTON, GEORGINA GLADYS, age 26; of 1 Hillsboro Road. 16 December 1942, at Bognor Regis War Memorial Hospital.

HOLLOWAY, ALBERT HARRY, age 51; Cpl., Home Guard; Firewatcher. Husband of K. E. Holloway, of 34 Havelock Road. 11 April 1941, at Havelock Road.

HUNNABALL, CECIL JAMES, age 60; of 3 Sudley House, Sudley Road. Husband of Gertrude Mary Hunnaball. 14 August 1942, at 44 Sudley Road.

LEACH, HERBERT EDWYN (FRANK HERBERT), age 40; of Malvern Close, Worthing. 14 August 1942, at Sudley Road.

MARTLEW, LEONARD, age 55; of 15 Beatty Road. Husband of Annie Martlew. 22 April 1943, at Beatty Road.

O'MALLEY, ADA MARY, age 68; of 46 Sudley Road. 14 August 1942, at Sudley Road.

RICHARDSON, GLADYS, age 33. Daughter of Fred and Fanny Richardson, of 97 Highfield Road. 28 November 1942, at Highfield Road.

ROBINSON, MAUD ELLEN, age 39; of Riber, Sturgess Road. Wife of Dvr. Edward George Alfred Robinson, Royal Army Service Corps. 14 August 1942, at Riber, Sturgess Road.

ROBINSON, SUSAN, age 80; of Riber, Sturgess Road. Widow of Authur John Robinson. 14 August 1942, at Riber, Sturgess Road.

SCOWEN, STANLEY RICHARD, age 11. Son of H.H. and B. Scowen, of 1 Southover Road. Injured 14 September 1940, at Sudley Lodge; died 25 September 1940, at Bognor Regis War Memorial Hospital.

WILLIAMS, AMY, age 64; of The Laurels, Sudley Road. 14 August 1942, at The Laurels, Sudley Road.

AIRCRAFT LOSSES IN AND AROUND BOGNOR

7. 7.1940	Hurricane	Lidsey Bridge
22. 7.1940	Hurricane	Morells Farm, Lagness
16. 8.1940	Junkers 87	Bowley Farm, S. Mundham
18. 8.1940	Hurricane	Summer Lane, Nyetimber
18. 8.1940	Spitfire	Elmers Sands
19. 8.1940	Spitfire	Colworth
26. 8.1940	Spitfire	Off Bognor Pier
9. 9.1940	Junkers 88	Pagham Harbour
10. 9.1940	Spitfire	Felpham Golf Course
30.10.1940	Blenheim	Orchard Way, South Bersted
15.11.1940	Me.109	Foreshore, Felpham
2. 2.1941	Hurricane	Morells Farm, Lagness
21. 7.1941	Spitfire	Oldlands Farm, Shripney
21. 7.1941	Spitfire	In sea off Bognor
5.10.1941	Spitfire	Bowley Farm, S. Mundham
5.10.1941	Spitfire	Sefter Farm, Nyetimber
10. 2.1942	Dornier 217	Lagness
14. 4.1942	Hampden	Sea Road, Felpham
4. 6.1942	Hurricane	Nr. Bognor Gas Works
28. 8.1942	Boston	Comet Corner, Middleton
26.10.1942	Beaufighter	The Sands, Middleton-on-Sea
16.12.1942	Dornier 217	Bognor Gas Works
14. 3.1943	Spitfire	In sea off Bognor
22. 4.1943	Typhoon	Beatty Road
24. 4.1943	Hampden	Lidsey
19. 6.1943	Typhoon	Pagham Harbour
7. 9.1943	Spitfire	Lidsey
15.10.1943	Typhoon	Shripney
30.11.1943	Mosquito	Off shore, Felpham
23. 1.1944	Spitfire	Pagham Harbour
30. 1.1944	Mosquito	Bilsham Corner
9. 2.1944	P51 Mustang	In sea off Bognor
24. 2.1944	Heinkel 177	In sea off Bognor
28. 2.1944	Mosquito	Bowley Farm, S. Mundham
20. 5.1944	Thunderbolt	Shripney
8. 6.1944	Spitfire	Flansham
4. 7.1944	B17 Fortress	Downview Road, Felpham
11. 9.1944	Typhoon	North Bersted

THE STATISTICS

1940

Alerts	350
Incidents	33
Bombs	126
U.X.B.	8
Incendiaries	400
Oil Bombs	7
Killed	3
Injured	18
Houses Damaged	169
Houses Demolished	11
Persons re-housed	7

1941

Alerts	441
Incidents	16
Bombs	86
Parachute Mines	7
U.X.B.	4
Incendiaries	200
Killed	8
Injured	22
Houses Damaged	360
Houses Demolished	15
Persons re-housed	65

1942

Alerts	193
Incidents	12
Bombs	22
U.X.B.	5
Incendiaries	50
Persons Killed	18
Persons Injured	78
Houses Damaged	1250
Houses Demolished	23
Persons re-housed	171

1943

Alerts	177
Incidents	6
Bombs	4
U.X.B.	8
Incendiaries	–
Sea Mines	5
Persons Killed	5
Persons Injured	70
Houses Damaged	872
Houses Demolished	7
Persons re-housed	31

1944

Alerts	130
Incidents	15
Bombs	n/k
U.X.B.	n/k
Incendiaries	n/k
Flying Bombs	1
Killed	1
Injured	65
Houses Damaged	565
Houses Demolished	4
Persons re-housed	n/k

NOTE:- The above statistics are compiled from data contained in the document "Bombs on Bognor" held by WSCC Records Office and the Libraries Service. The total of persons killed (35) does not correspond to the total recorded in Civilian War Death Registers for Bognor Regis by the Commonwealth War Graves Commission which show 22 fatalities. It is possible that the figure of 35 includes service war deaths in Bognor Regis in addition to the 22 civilians.

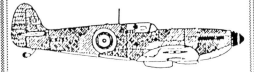